Planes and
Other
Flying Things

•FLORENCE TEMKO•

The Millbrook Press
Brookfield, Connecticut

Published in the United States in 1996 by
The Millbrook Press, Inc.
2 Old New Milford Road
Brookfield, Connecticut 06804

First published in Great Britain in 1995 by
Dragon's World Limited
7 St. George's Square, London SWIV 2HX

© 1995 Dragon's World
Text and paper project designs
  © 1995 Florence Temko

Text: Florence Temko
Editor: Kyla Barber
Design: Mel Raymond, Bob Scott
Illustrations: John Walls
Art Director: John Strange
Editorial Director: Pippa Rubinstein

Library of Congress Cataloging-in-Publication Data
Temko, Florence.
  Paper magic. Planes and other flying things / by Florence Temko.
      p. cm.
  Includes bibliographical references and index.
  Summary: Presents simple instructions for folding paper to make airplanes and other flying things including the glider, star ship, helicopter, pterosaur, and even the Concorde.
  ISBN 0-7613-0041-4 (lib. bdg.)
  ISBN 0-7613-0082-1 (pbk.)
    1. Paper airplanes--
         Juvenile literature.
    [1. Paper airplanes.
    2. Handicraft.]
    I. Title.
TL770.T39 1996
745.592--dc20

                96-4545
                 CIP
                 AC

Printed in Italy

CONTENTS

One, two, or three planes next to a heading indicate the degree of difficulty.
Easy

You can do it

For aircraft engineers!

INTRODUCTION

Paper aircraft are easy to construct and fun to fly. Perhaps you already know how to make one or two, but in this book you can find out how to make many others. You will also find ideas about how you can change them to fly better and how to have contests with your friends.

The book starts with instructions for the Glider, which is the most popular paper aircraft, and it is followed by the Star Ship. They show how you can play with the basic pattern.

After that, you can find out how to make many other types of paper planes, and how to build an airport and a mobile. You can change the designs as you please.

You can make most planes from notebook or typing paper. If you decorate them with markers you can give them your own personal design.

PAPER TO USE

Most of the planes shown in this book can be made from standard letter-sized (8½ x 11-inch) paper. It may be typing, notebook, or computer paper. If a special type of paper is required you will find it noted under **You will need** at the beginning of the directions. Origami paper is useful for planes that begin with a square.

KEY TO SYMBOLS

Crease paper up (valley fold)

– – – – – – – – – – – – –

A crease made before

———————————

Cut

——————————— ✂

Arrow points in the direction in which the paper is to be folded

Double arrow means fold and then unfold the crease

Turn the paper over from back to front

HOW TO CUT A SQUARE

1 Crease the corner of a sheet of paper in half by bringing the short edge to the long edge.

2 Cut off the single layer of paper.

3 Here is the square.

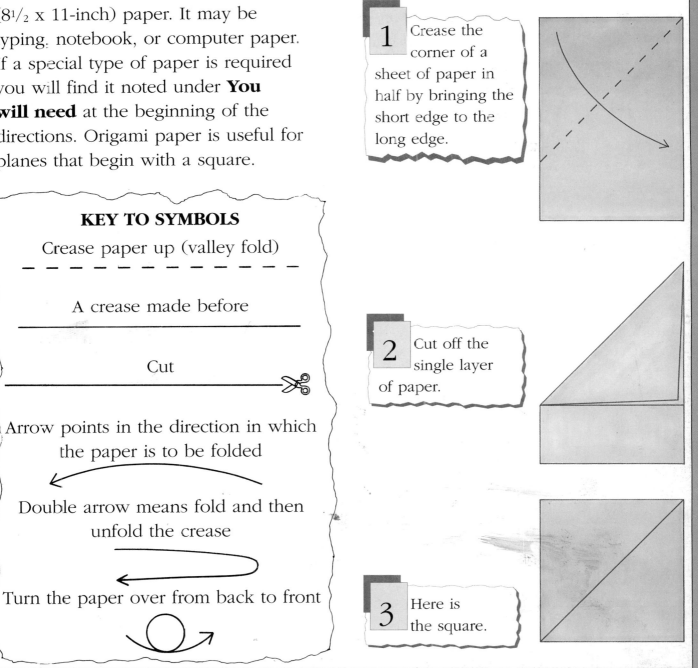

ABOUT AERODYNAMICS

Have you ever wondered why a heavy plane can fly through the air? It's because of aerodynamics. Aerodynamics describe the movement of air around an aircraft, and explain how the wings of a plane are designed so that movement forward can produce movement up.

Here are some definitions of words used in the science of aerodynamics which apply to paper planes, too:

Ailerons: Any movable tabs that control sideways balance.

Biplane: A plane with two sets of wings, one above the other. The upper one is usually placed slightly forward.

Drag: The air resistance that slows the plane's movement forward.

Elevators: Movable parts, usually near the tail of the plane. *See Tabs.*

Fuselage: The body of the plane to which the wings, engines, and other parts are attached.

Gravity: The force which attracts bodies to the Earth—and keeps our feet on the ground!

Keel: The part of the plane under the wings. It provides stability.

Leading Edge: The front edge of the wings.

Lift: The force that causes the plane to rise.

Monoplane: A plane with one set of wings.

Nose: The front point of the plane.

Rudder: A vertical part of the tail that makes the plane turn right or left.

Slats: Bending the outer tips of the wings up. They should not be completely upright but leaning to the outside.

Tabs: Sections at the back of the wing that can be bent up or down. (In paper planes they can be created with two small cuts.) Tabs can help a plane to climb or dive. For example, experiment with tabs if your plane dives into the ground instead of flying straight ahead.

Tail: The back of the plane.

Thrust: The force that pushes the plane forward.

Trim: If a plane tends to dive down, bend up the tail to improve flight. Experiment by cutting tabs (*see definition*) for added performance.

Wind direction: If you fly your plane outdoors, let it fly in the same direction as the wind is blowing.

Wings: They provide lift.

GENERAL FLYING HELP

Any paper plane can be launched to go forward for a distance. A really good plane seems to be lifted, and floats in the air for at least a moment. That's what gives you the thrill of flying paper planes. Follow the step-by-step directions for each design in this book and try to improve its flight.

How to launch planes

It is usually best to release a plane gently, not with a jerk. Hold it under the wings; push and release it in an upward path.

Add a paper clip

Sometimes a plane flies better when weight is added to its nose. You can achieve this by attaching a paper clip. It also keeps the layers of paper together, reducing air resistance. Try moving the paper clip to different positions.

Add tape

Tape keeps the layers of paper together without adding the weight of a paper clip.

Tabs

Some paper planes fly better with tabs. Make them with two 1/2-inch (1-centimeter) cuts on the back of each wing. Bend the tabs up slightly.

Experiment

By changing the direction of the launch:
Up into the air or straight ahead.
By holding the plane in different launching positions: Shift your hand along the body of the plane under the wings.
By adjusting the wings up and down.
By bending or cutting tabs (ailerons) at the back of the wing: If you want your plane to climb more, move the tabs up. If you want it to dive more, move them down.

DECORATIONS

After you have folded a plane you can decorate it with colored pens. Make it as colorful as you like. You can also add stickers, but they may change the way the plane flies.

GAMES AND CONTESTS

It's fun to fly planes with your friends. Here are some ideas you can try:
Sample rules to be set before games or contests start:

- everyone folds the same type of plane
- everyone can fly any kind of plane
- make some design changes to one of the planes in this book
- invent a new plane

Have a contest. Declare winners for different results:

- the plane that flew the longest distance
- the plane that stayed in the air the longest time
- the plane that looped the best
- the plane that landed on a set target (a big circle, for example)

THE GLIDER

Most people know the glider. It's not only easy to fold, but flies well, too.

You will need
*Letter size paper,
8½ x 11 inches*

1 Fold the paper in half lengthwise. Unfold the paper so it lies flat.

2 At one end, fold the corners to the crease.

3 Bring the slanted, folded edge to the long crease.

4 Bring the folded edges to the middle again. TURN THE PAPER OVER.

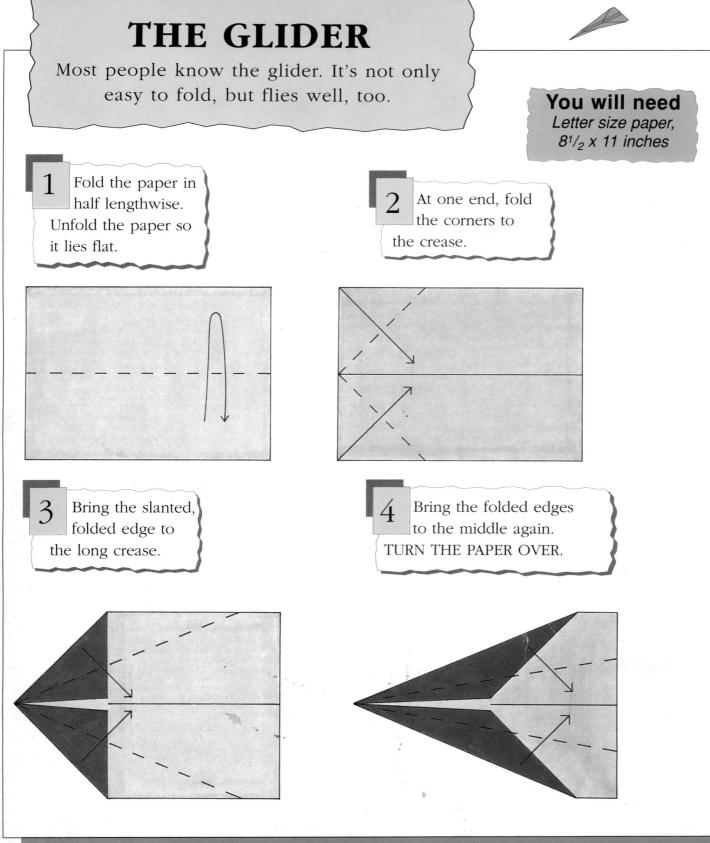

5 Fold the plane in half lengthwise.

6 Loosen the wings to stick out to the sides. Hold the plane from below. Launch it slightly upwards.

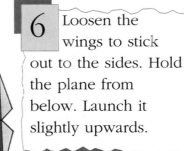

7 The Glider.

Add some string

Every time you launch your glider, you have to run to pick it up. If you attach a string, you can stay where you are and pull it in.

You will need
Your glider
Kite string
Stapler, hole puncher

1. Punch a hole near the back of the plane. Tie on the kite string.
2. Launch the glider with one hand. Hold the end of the string with the other hand.
3. After its flight pull in the glider with the string.

No hole puncher?

Use the point of a pair of scissors.

Flying help

The Glider flies well without much help, but you can move the wings up or down a little. Attach a paper clip.

STAR SHIP

Some changes on the popular glider produce a different silhouette altogether.

You will need
Letter or notebook paper
Tape

1 Fold the paper in half lengthwise. Unfold.

2 Fold the top corners to the crease.

3 Bring the slanted, folded edge to the long crease.

4 Reach inside on the left and pull out the hidden corner of the paper.

5 Fold the corner over to the other side.

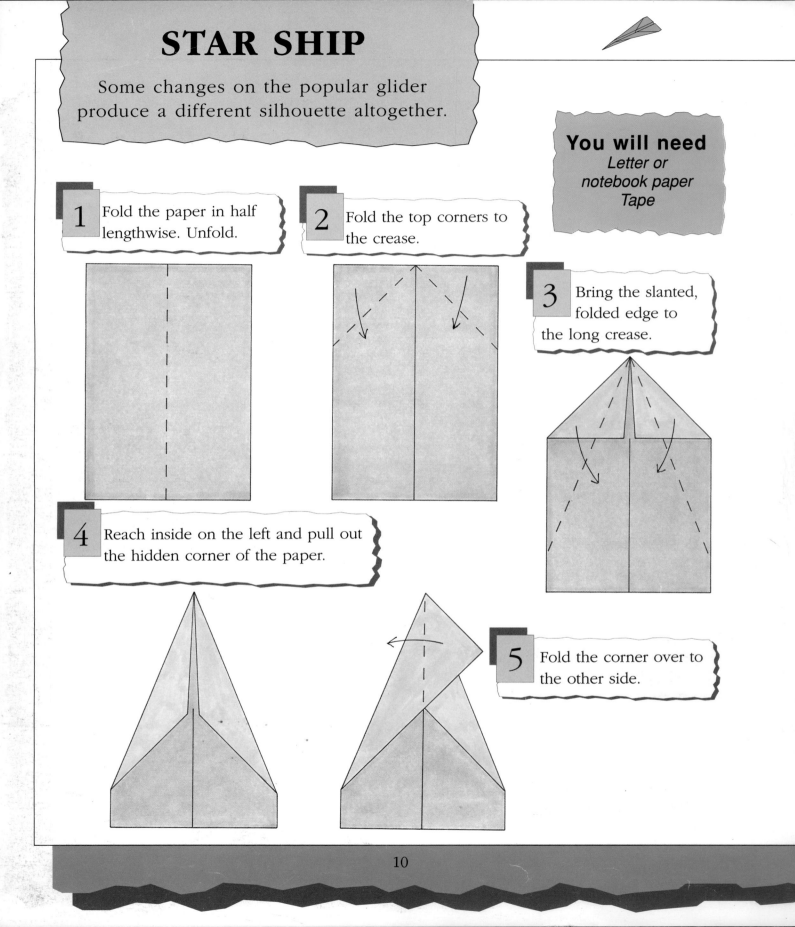

6 Repeat steps 4 and 5 with the other hidden corner on the right.

7 Fold the top corner down.

8 Fold the glider in half.

9 On the front, fold the long slanted edge to the bottom edge. See next drawing. Repeat this on the back.

TAPE

10 Loosen the wings to stick out to the sides. Put a piece of tape where shown. Hold the plane near its nose and throw it slightly up.

Flying help
The Star Ship flies well without much help, but you can move the wings up or down a little.

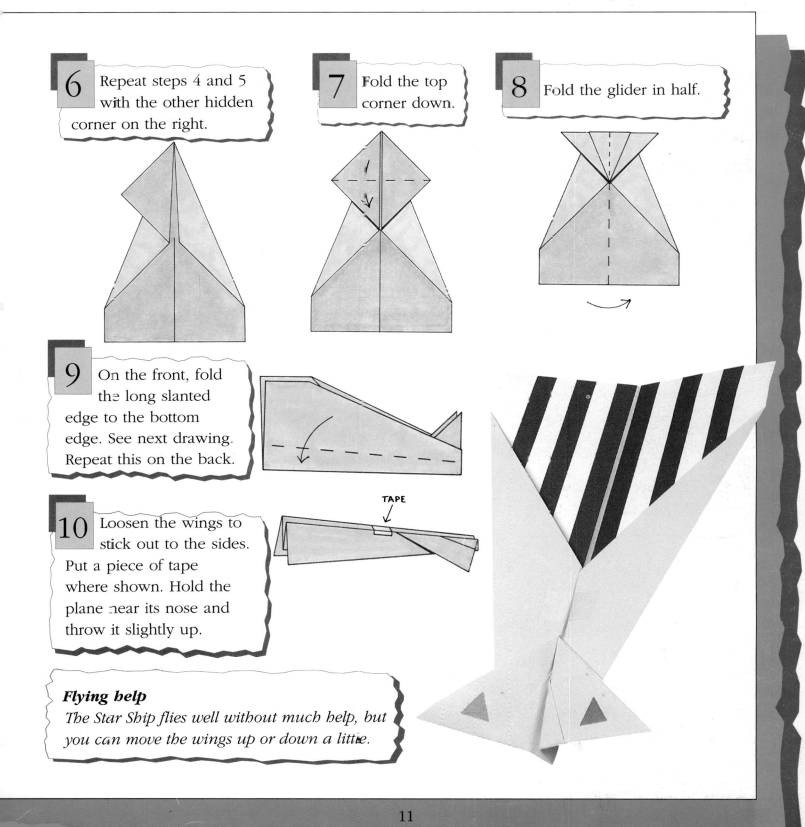

FLYING PELICAN

The Flying Pelican has the long beak of a real pelican. It is made by adding a few folds to the basic Glider (see page 8). They add weight to the front, which helps it fly even better.

You will need
Letter or notebook paper

1 Fold the paper in half lengthwise. Unfold.

2 Fold the top corners to the crease.

3 Bring the slanted, folded edge to the long crease.

4 Fold the pointed nose to X.

6 Fold the plane in half.

5 Fold the nose up again, making a pleat about $1/2$ inch (1 centimeter) wide.

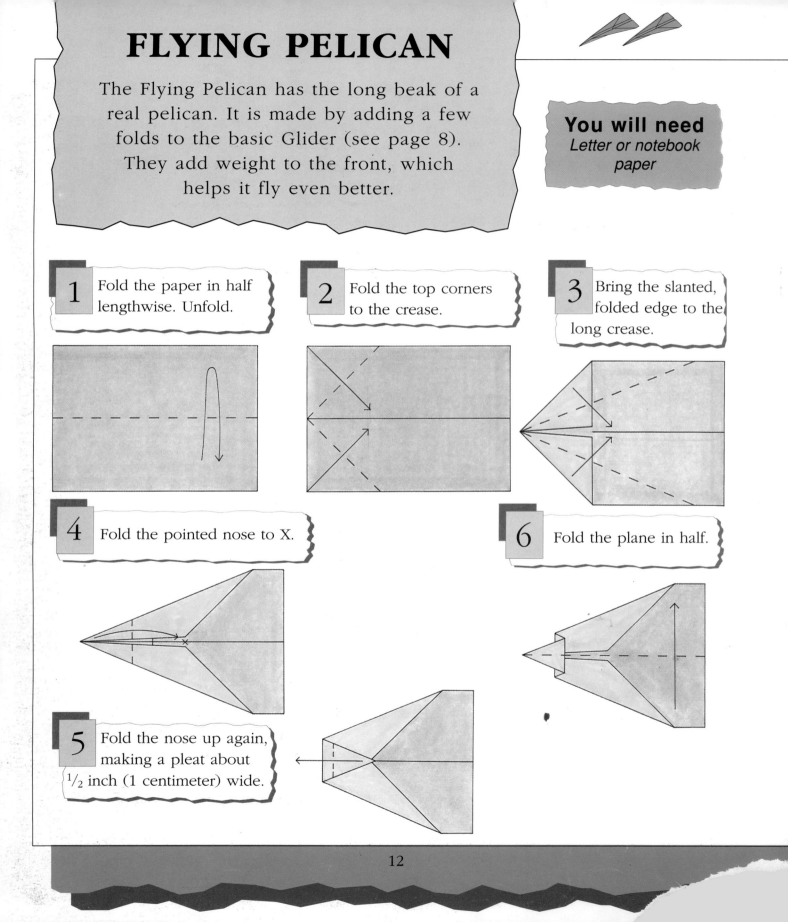

7 Fold the wings down on both sides, leaving the head alone. As you do this, the paper forms a triangle at the front of the wing. See the next drawing.

8 Loosen the wings to stick out to the sides. Hold the pelican behind the pleat and throw it slightly up.

triangle forms here

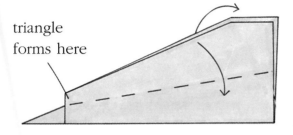

9 Flying Pelican.

Flying help

The Flying Pelican needs little help to fly well, but you can move the wings up or down slightly.

BLUNT NOSE

This plane has slats on the wings for better flight.

You will need
Letter or notebook paper

1 Fold the top edge to the side edge.

2 Fold down the top corner.

3 Fold down the new top corner.

4 Fold the plane in half.

5 Fold down the wings on the front and on the back.

6 Fold up the bottom edges on the front and back to make slats. Let the wings stick out to the sides. Let the slats stick straight up.

7 Blunt Nose Plane.

Flying help
Hold the plane near the nose and push it gently into an upward path.

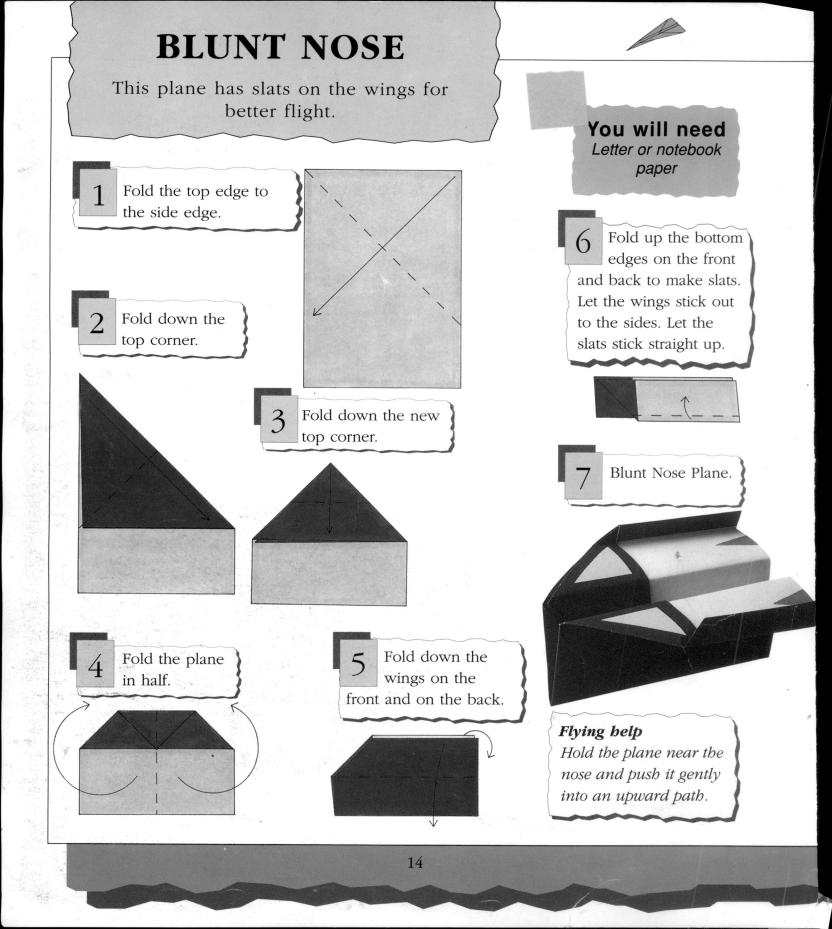

FLYING SAUCER

It's so easy to make a Flying Saucer. You'll wonder why you've never made one before.

You will need
2 paper plates
Tape or stapler

1 Place the two plates together with the bulges facing out.

2 Bind the edges together with a stapler or tape. Place the edges of the plates in the middle of the tape and push over the sides of the tape. That's the easiest way to get it even.

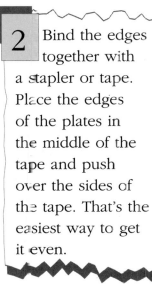

3 Flying Saucer.

Launching

Launch the saucer by holding it by the edge and flicking your wrist. Experiment with different ways of throwing it.
See who can throw it furthest.

Decorate

The wilder the better, because nobody knows what Flying Saucers really look like. Experiment with all sorts of additions; stick some extra shapes on the top—control centers and living quarters for the aliens. But be careful, extra bits on the flying saucer might stop it from flying so well.

SIDEWAYS PLANE

The plane does not fly sideways, but you place the paper sideways before you begin folding.

You will need
*Letter or notebook paper
Tape*

1 Fold the paper in half the short way. Unfold it.

2 Fold the two top corners to the crease.

3 Bring the two loose edges to the slanted edges.

4 Fold the top corner down.

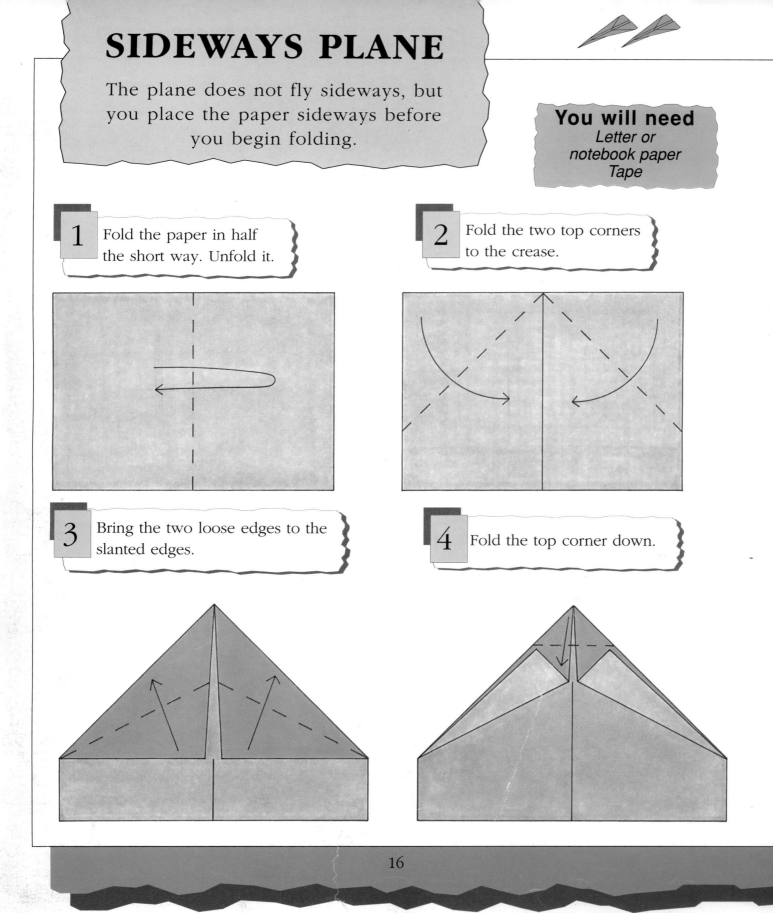

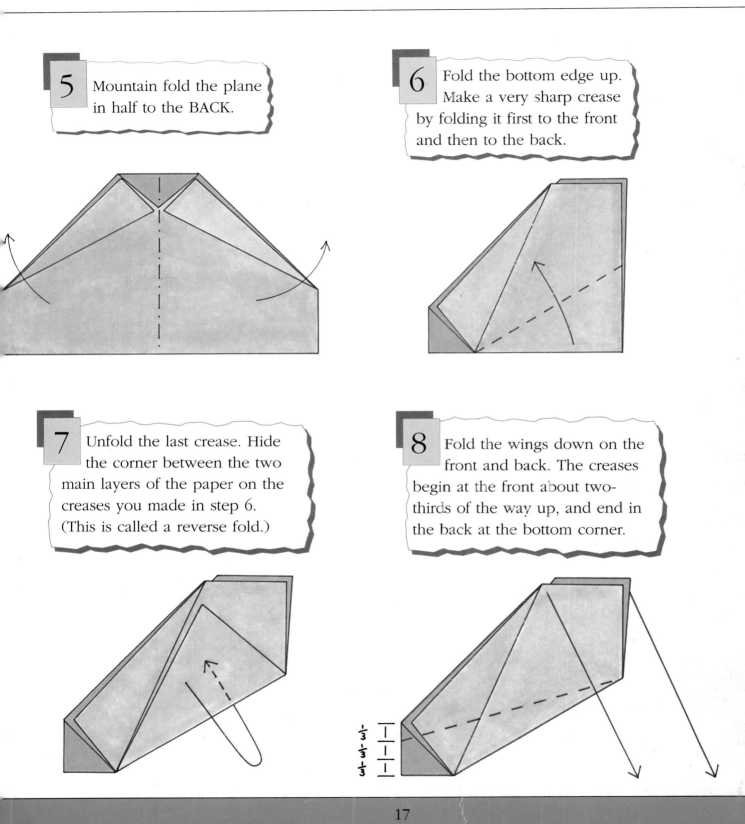

5 Mountain fold the plane in half to the BACK.

6 Fold the bottom edge up. Make a very sharp crease by folding it first to the front and then to the back.

7 Unfold the last crease. Hide the corner between the two main layers of the paper on the creases you made in step 6. (This is called a reverse fold.)

8 Fold the wings down on the front and back. The creases begin at the front about two-thirds of the way up, and end in the back at the bottom corner.

$\frac{1}{3}$
$\frac{1}{3}$
$\frac{1}{3}$

9 Fold the rudder down with a very sharp crease. Then hide half of the rudder in between two layers of paper on the same creases. (This is another reverse fold.)

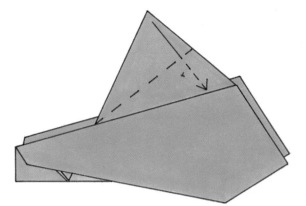

10 Loosen the wings out to the sides. Place a piece of tape on top of the plane.

Flying help
Experiment with placing pieces of tape in different spots on the top of the plane or on the nose.

11 Sideways Plane.

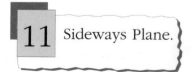

SPACE ROCKET

Use this simple space rocket for birthday and other party decorations. Metallic papers are best.

You will need
*Letter or notebook paper
Pencil, scissors*

1 Fold the paper in half.

2 Fold it in half again.

3 Draw half a rocket at the double folded edge, as shown. Cut on the pencil line.

4 You now have two rocket shapes. Cut halfway down the middle of one. Cut halfway up the middle of the other.

5 Slide the two pieces together at the cuts. To make them stand up, arrange them at right angles to each other.

6 Space Rocket.

You could make your own launch pad, too!

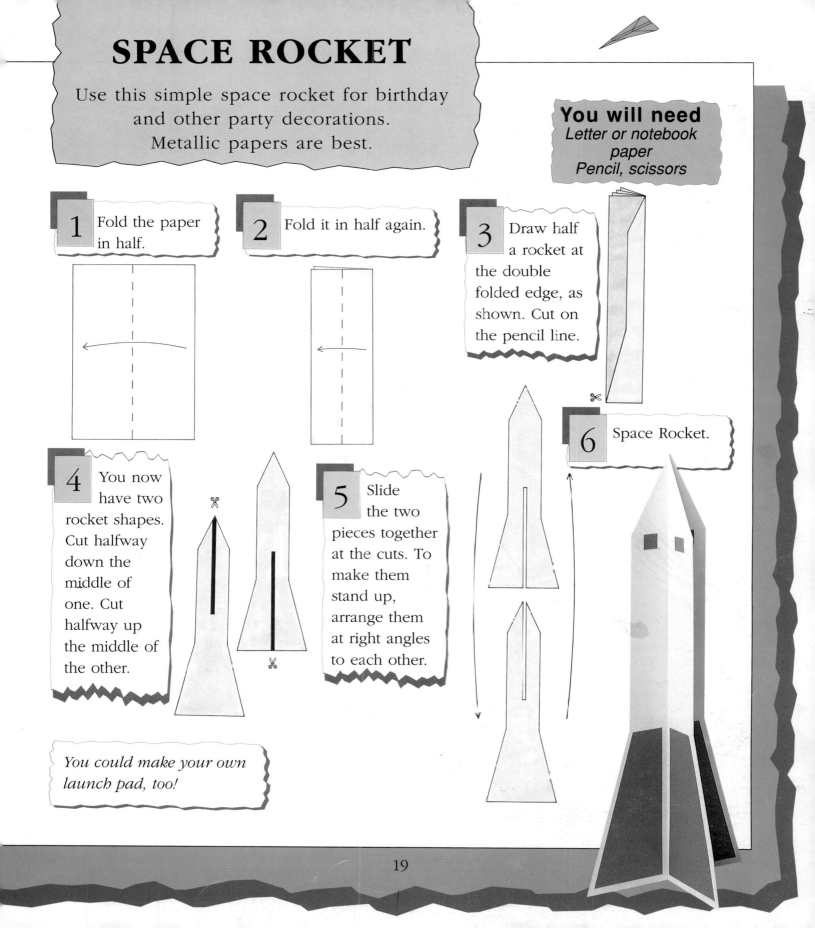

ORIGAMI PLANE

Fold this plane from a square of paper, not a rectangle. It's a good flyer.

You will need
A paper square
(see page 5)

1 Fold the square from corner to corner. Unfold the paper so it lies flat.

2 Bring the ends of the crease together and make a small mark at the middle.

3 Fold the top corner to the mark.

4 Beginning at the left top corner, make a crease to bring the top edge to the middle.

5 Repeat on the right hand side.

6 Unfold the creases made in steps 4 and 5.

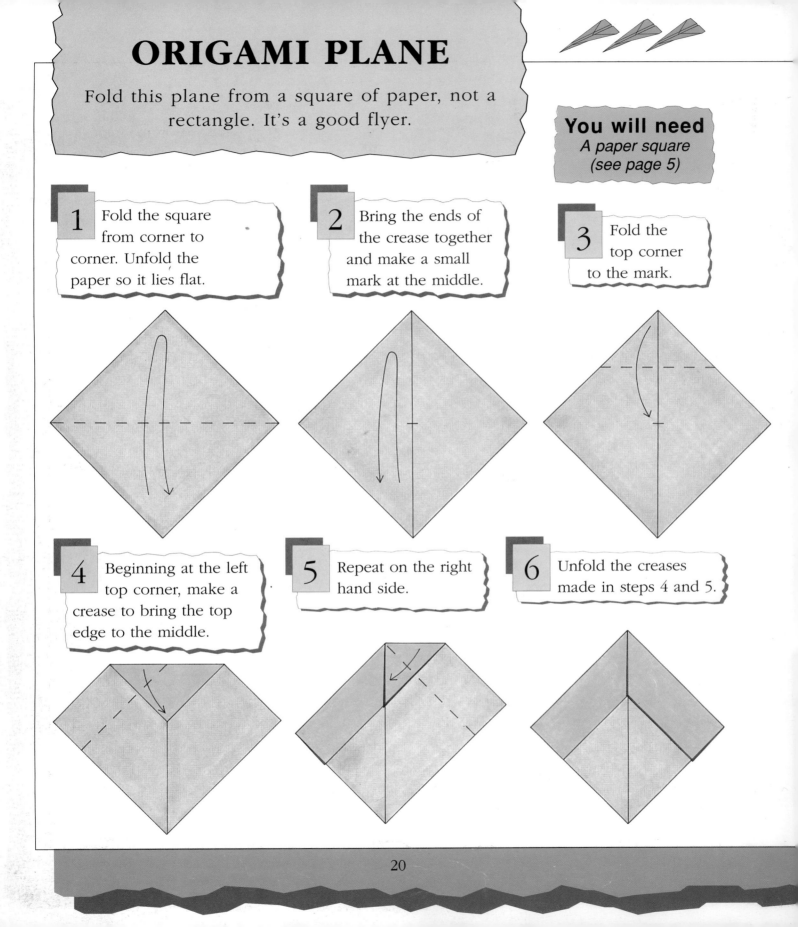

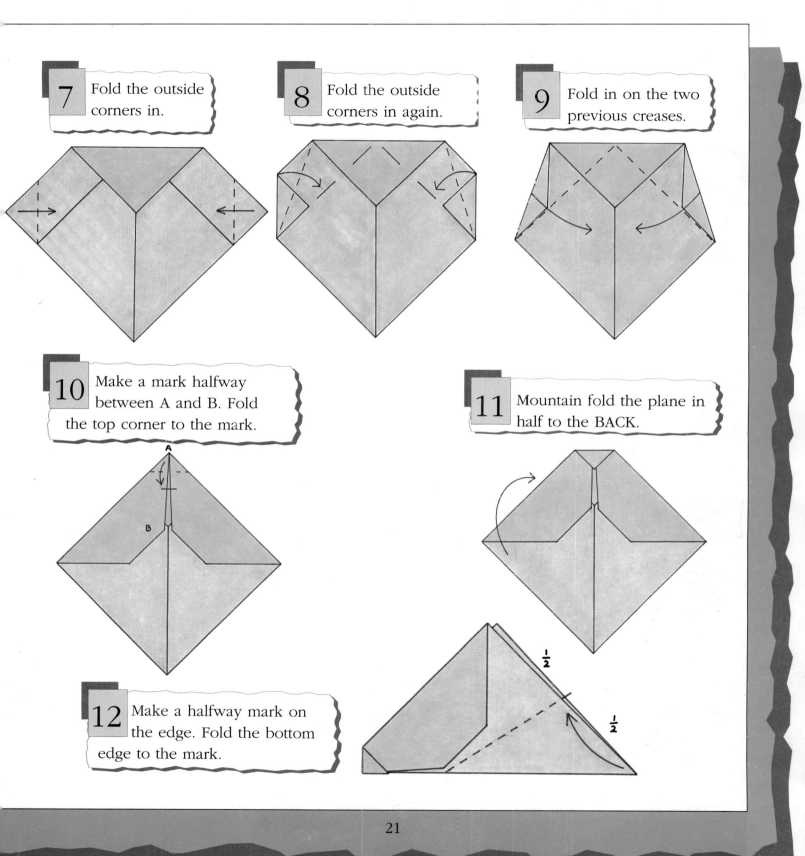

7 Fold the outside corners in.

8 Fold the outside corners in again.

9 Fold in on the two previous creases.

10 Make a mark halfway between A and B. Fold the top corner to the mark.

A

B

11 Mountain fold the plane in half to the BACK.

12 Make a halfway mark on the edge. Fold the bottom edge to the mark.

$\frac{1}{2}$

$\frac{1}{2}$

13 Unfold step 12. Reverse fold the paper in between the two main layers of paper using the existing creases.

14 Fold the wings out to the sides. The new creases are parallel to the short bottom edge.

15 Origami Plane.

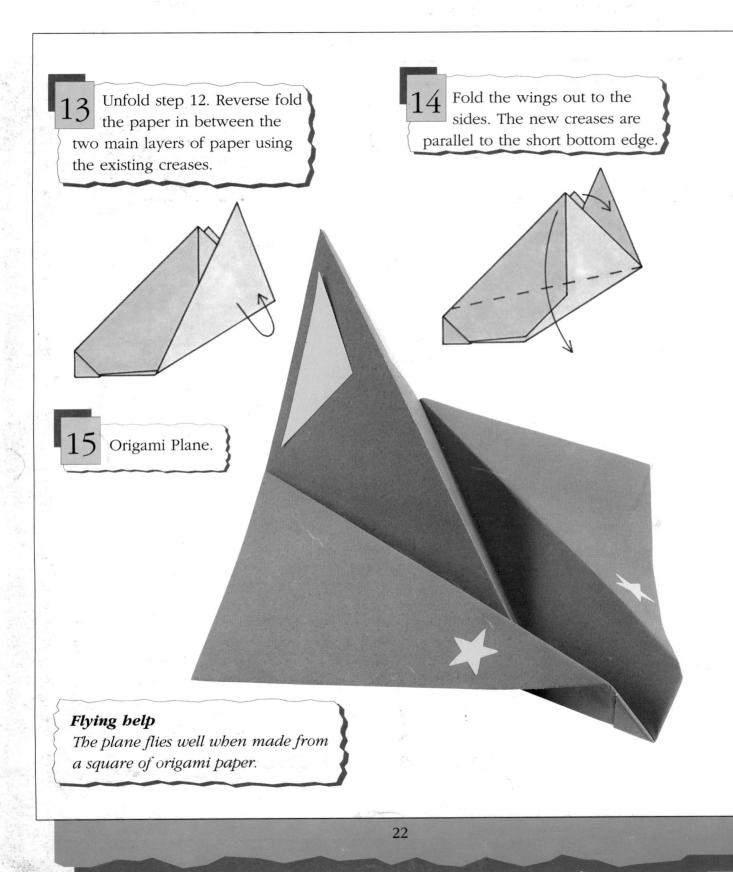

Flying help
The plane flies well when made from a square of origami paper.

HELICOPTER

It twirls and spins its blades when you release it from overhead.

You will need
A strip of paper,
3 x 8 inches (8 x 20 centimeters)
A paper clip
Scissors

1 Make a halfway mark on one of the long edges. Cut in $1/3$ of the way from both sides.

2 Fold both sides in, overlapping the paper. Put on a paper clip.

4 Helicopter.

3 Cut down from the top edge not all the way to the narrowed paper. Bend one of the blades to the front and the other one to the back.

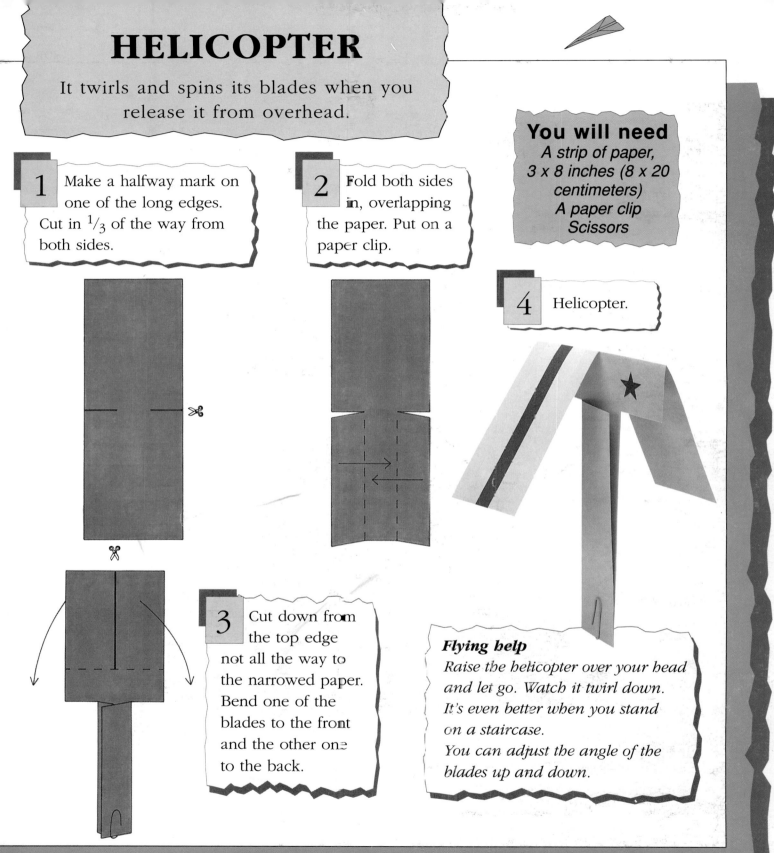

Flying help

Raise the helicopter over your head and let go. Watch it twirl down.
It's even better when you stand on a staircase.
You can adjust the angle of the blades up and down.

D-PLANE

One rainy afternoon when two cousins, David and Dennis, were ten years old, they made paper planes. After a while they invented a new plane and they decided to call it the D-Plane. It flies really well.

You will need
Letter or notebook paper
A paper clip

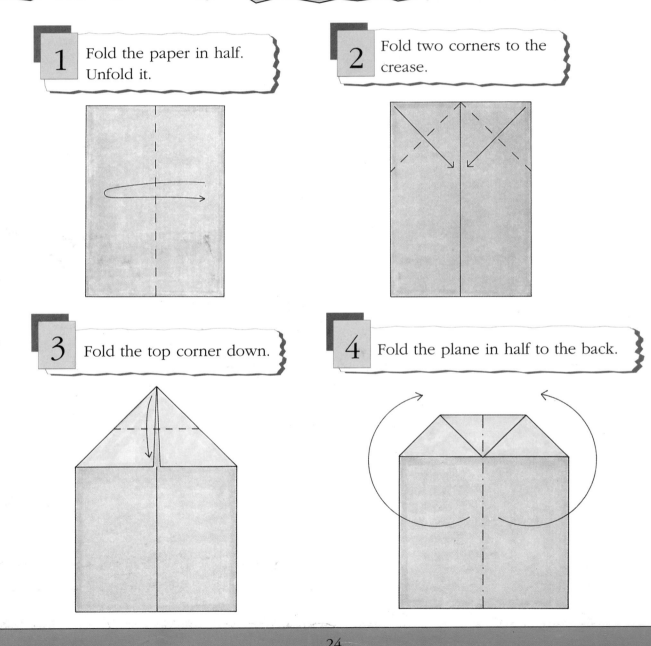

1 Fold the paper in half. Unfold it.

2 Fold two corners to the crease.

3 Fold the top corner down.

4 Fold the plane in half to the back.

5 Fold the short front edge to the bottom edge. Do it on the front and then match the back.

6 Fold down the wings. The crease is made by placing the top corner on the bottom edge.

7 Place a paper clip on the nose. Loosen the wings.

8 D-Plane.

Maybe you can invent a plane, too.

GLOBAL FLYER

This smooth flying plane is popular all over the world.

You will need
Letter or notebook paper

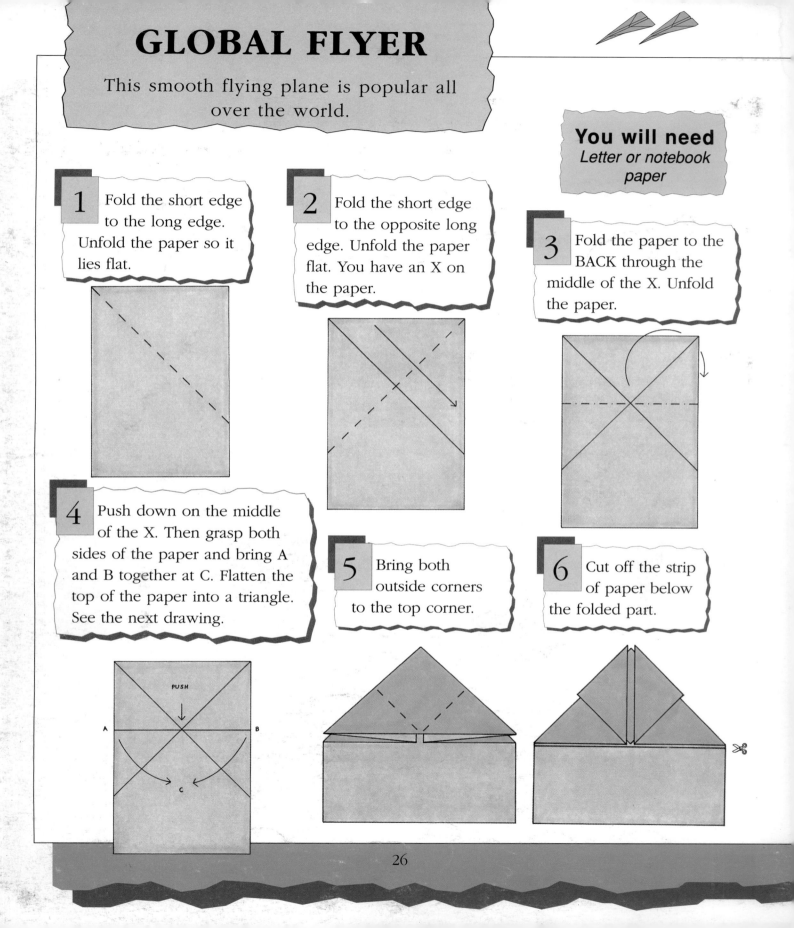

1 Fold the short edge to the long edge. Unfold the paper so it lies flat.

2 Fold the short edge to the opposite long edge. Unfold the paper flat. You have an X on the paper.

3 Fold the paper to the BACK through the middle of the X. Unfold the paper.

4 Push down on the middle of the X. Then grasp both sides of the paper and bring A and B together at C. Flatten the top of the paper into a triangle. See the next drawing.

5 Bring both outside corners to the top corner.

6 Cut off the strip of paper below the folded part.

PUSH

A   B

C

7 Cut the strip in half.

8 Fold one of the new strips in half and unfold it. Throw away the other strip.

9 Push the strip all the way up, inside the plane.

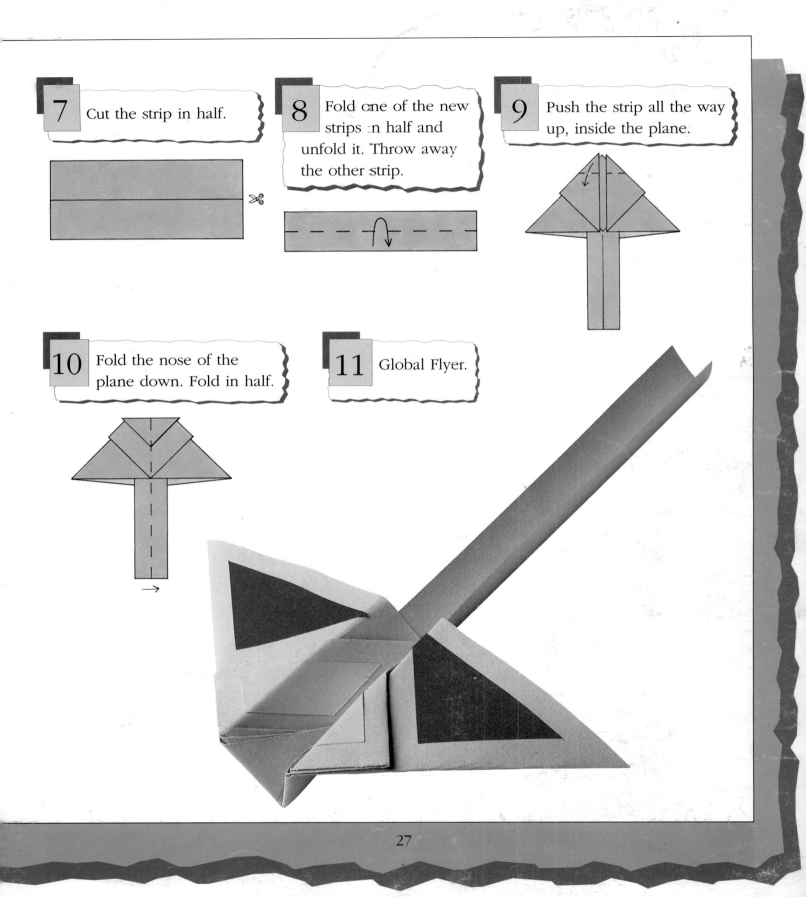

10 Fold the nose of the plane down. Fold in half.

11 Global Flyer.

PTEROSAUR

Pterosaurs glided and swooped in the air over sixty million years ago, while dinosaurs roamed the Earth. Pterosaurs were the largest flying creatures that ever existed. Their bodies measured about 30 feet (10 meters) and their wings were 50 feet (17 meters) across.

1 Fold the paper in half. Copy the outline of the pterosaur onto the paper. Make it as large as possible. The head and back feet lie on the folded edge. Cut on the outline through both layers. Do not cut away the folded edge at the head and the back feet as they hold the mobile together. Color both sides with felt-tip pens. No one really knows what color the dinosaurs were; what color do you think they might have been?

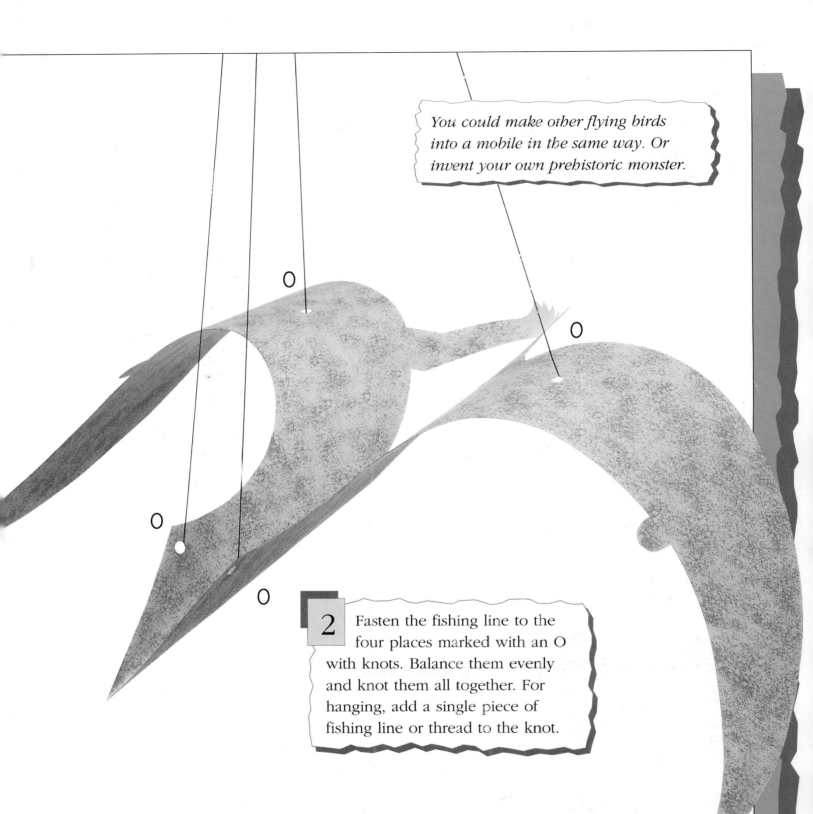

You could make other flying birds into a mobile in the same way. Or invent your own prehistoric monster.

O

O

O

O

2 Fasten the fishing line to the four places marked with an O with knots. Balance them evenly and knot them all together. For hanging, add a single piece of fishing line or thread to the knot.

FLYING WING

Imagine a plane which has only two wings but no body. It's called a Flying Wing. When it was built experimentally it performed well, but it was never produced. Flying Wings are still the dreams of some aircraft designers and the planes may possibly be built in the future. Meanwhile, it is very simple to make one with paper, and it flies beautifully.

You will need
Letter or notebook paper
A paper clip

1 Place the paper with the long edge at the top.

Fold it in half and unfold it again

2 Fold the top corners to the middle crease.

3 Fold the top corner down.

4 Fold the slanted edges to the middle.

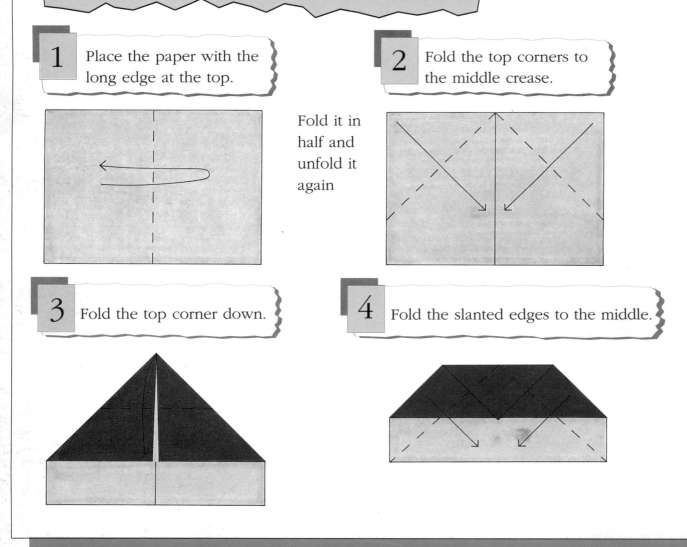

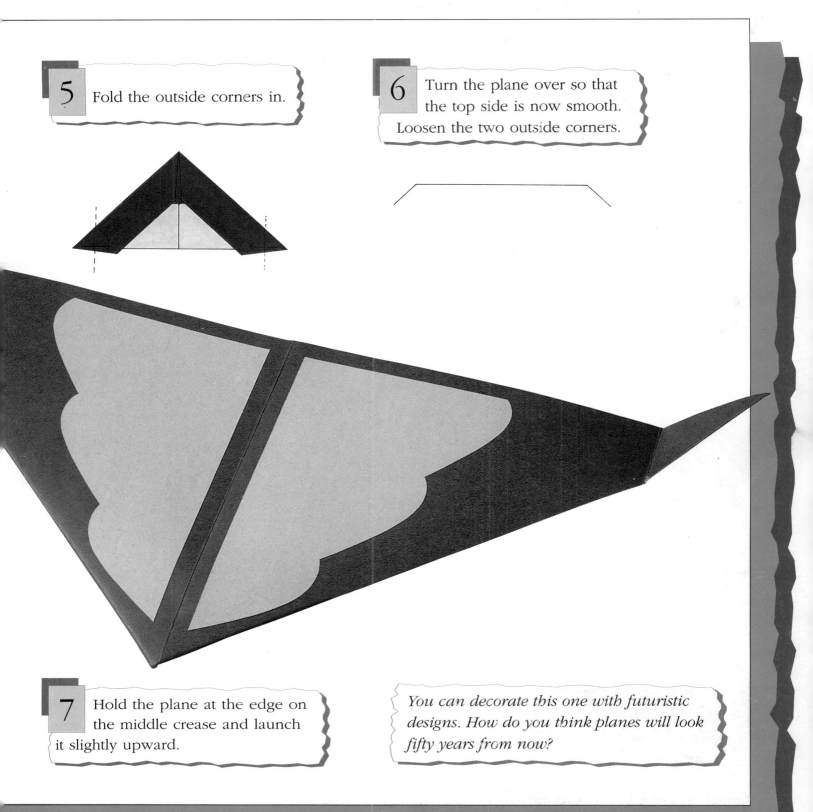

5 Fold the outside corners in.

6 Turn the plane over so that the top side is now smooth. Loosen the two outside corners.

7 Hold the plane at the edge on the middle crease and launch it slightly upward.

You can decorate this one with futuristic designs. How do you think planes will look fifty years from now?

HYDROPLANE

A real hydroplane is a mixture of plane and boat constructions. It is propelled by strong air jets forced from its underside to keep it skimming over water. When you blow on the back of a paper hydroplane, it will skim along a table top.

The hydroplane requires many steps—but it's worth it! Follow the instructions carefully, and make sure that you turn the plane from front to back at the right times.

You will need
Letter or notebook paper

1 Cut the paper in half lengthwise. Each piece makes one hydroplane.

2 Fold the short edge to the long edge. Unfold the paper so that it lies flat.

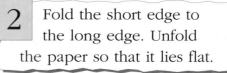

3 Fold the short edge to the opposite long edge. Unfold the paper again so that it lies flat. You have an X on the paper.

4 Fold the paper to the BACK through the middle of the X. Unfold the paper.

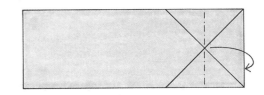

5 Push down on the middle of the X. Then bring A and B together at C. Flatten the top of the paper into a triangle. See the next drawing.

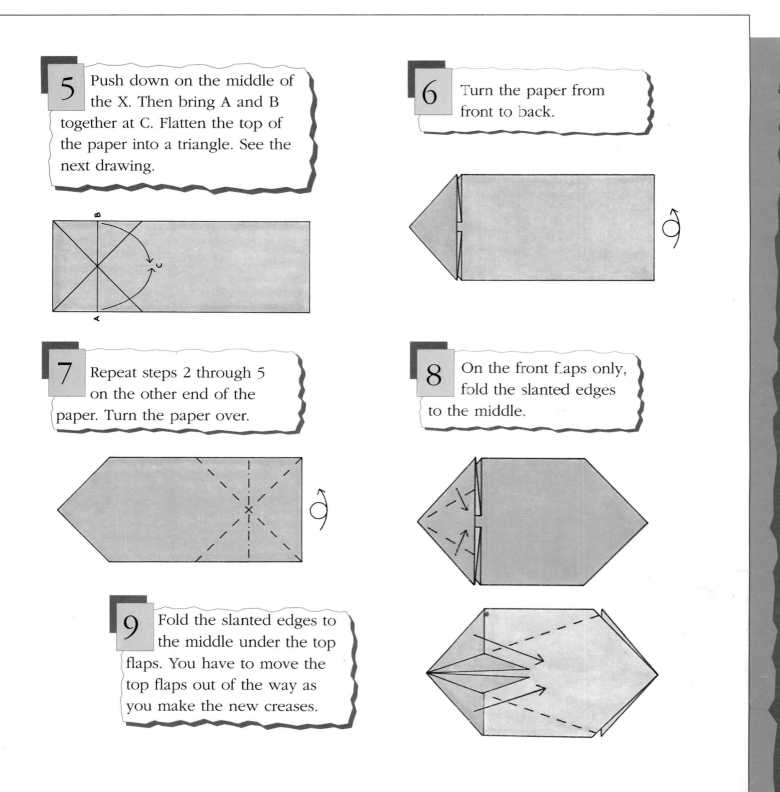

6 Turn the paper from front to back.

7 Repeat steps 2 through 5 on the other end of the paper. Turn the paper over.

8 On the front flaps only, fold the slanted edges to the middle.

9 Fold the slanted edges to the middle under the top flaps. You have to move the top flaps out of the way as you make the new creases.

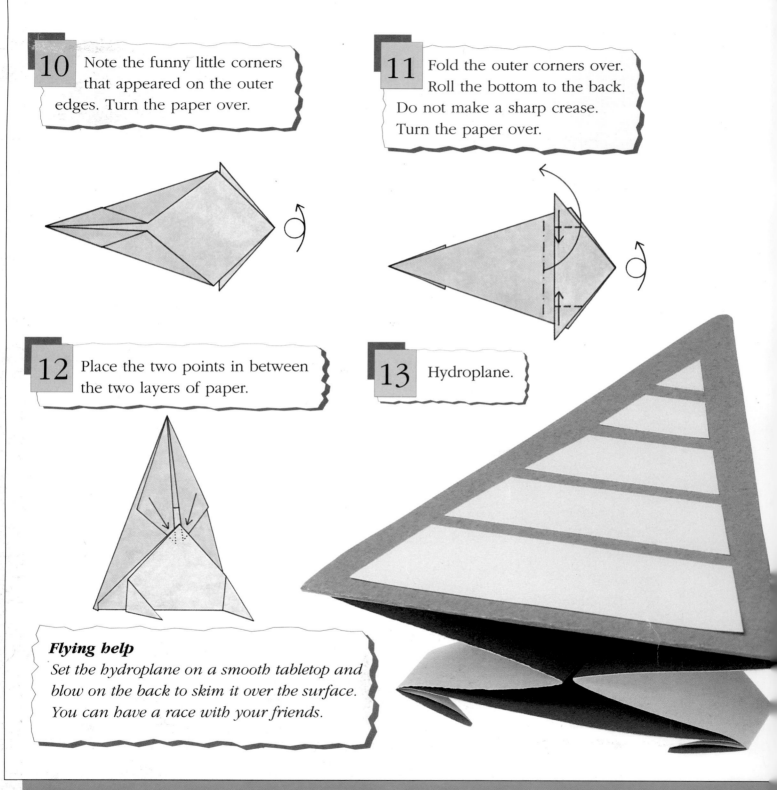

10 Note the funny little corners that appeared on the outer edges. Turn the paper over.

11 Fold the outer corners over. Roll the bottom to the back. Do not make a sharp crease. Turn the paper over.

12 Place the two points in between the two layers of paper.

13 Hydroplane.

Flying help

Set the hydroplane on a smooth tabletop and blow on the back to skim it over the surface. You can have a race with your friends.

WIND DARTER

Designed by Michael Weinstein

The streamlined Wind Darter may be one of your favorite planes as you send it soaring into the air. The designer is an expert paper folder who created it within the rules of origami, which forbid any cutting or gluing. At first, follow the instructions slowly and carefully. After a while, and with a little practice, you can fold it up in two minutes.

You will need
A square of origami or other lightweight paper
Pencil

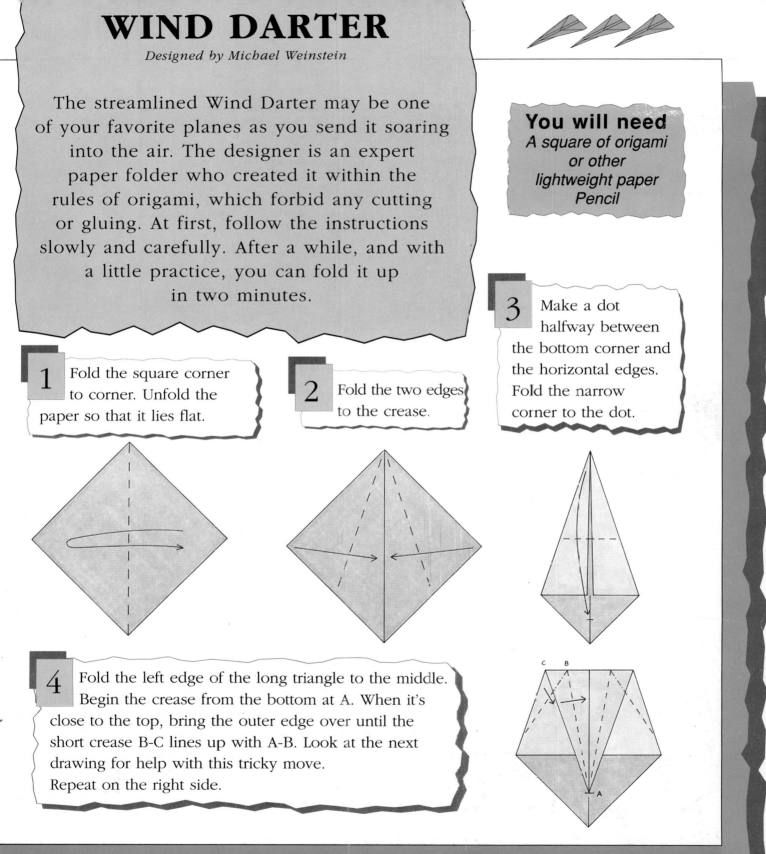

1 Fold the square corner to corner. Unfold the paper so that it lies flat.

2 Fold the two edges to the crease.

3 Make a dot halfway between the bottom corner and the horizontal edges. Fold the narrow corner to the dot.

4 Fold the left edge of the long triangle to the middle. Begin the crease from the bottom at A. When it's close to the top, bring the outer edge over until the short crease B-C lines up with A-B. Look at the next drawing for help with this tricky move.
Repeat on the right side.

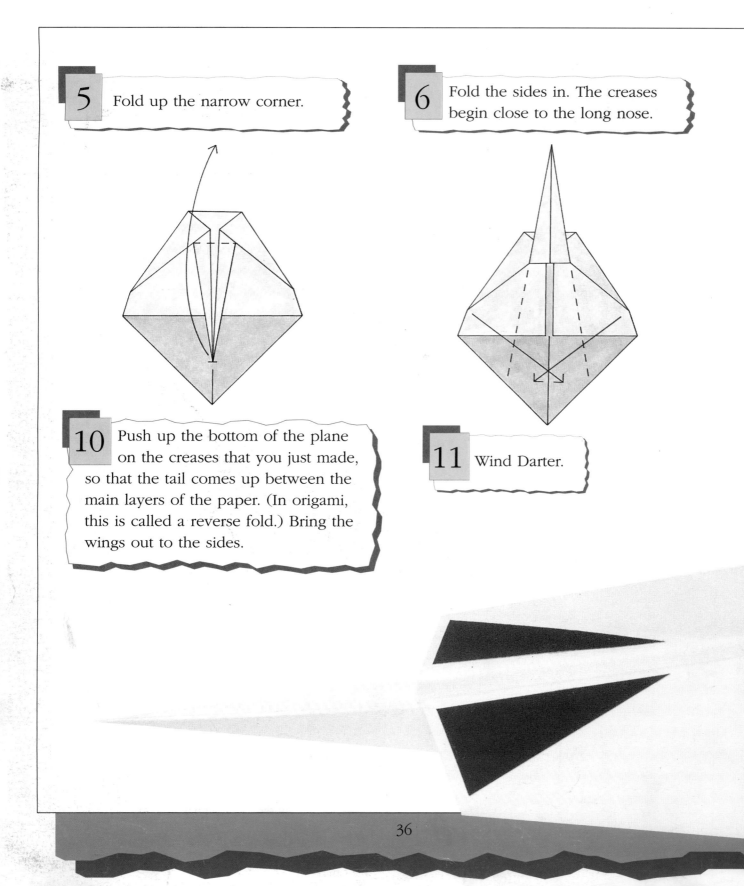

5 Fold up the narrow corner.

6 Fold the sides in. The creases begin close to the long nose.

10 Push up the bottom of the plane on the creases that you just made, so that the tail comes up between the main layers of the paper. (In origami, this is called a reverse fold.) Bring the wings out to the sides.

11 Wind Darter.

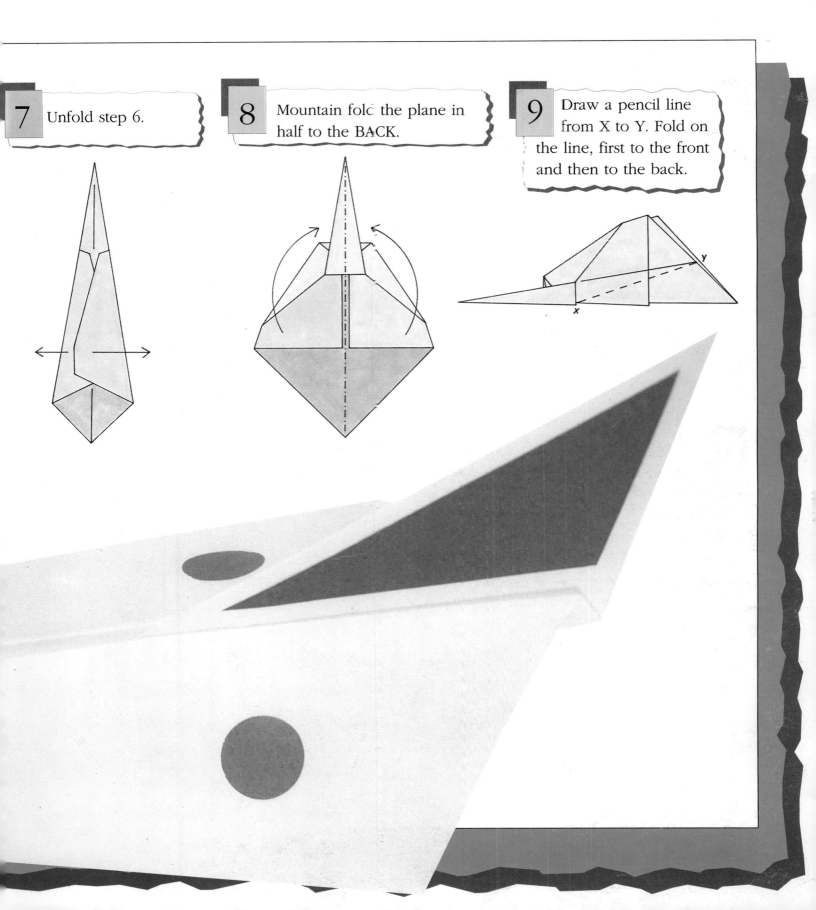

7 Unfold step 6.

8 Mountain fold the plane in half to the BACK.

9 Draw a pencil line from X to Y. Fold on the line, first to the front and then to the back.

CONCORDE

Designed by Thay Yang, author of Exotic Paper Airplanes, *and a winner in the Great International Paper Airplane Contest when he was 14 years old.*

The supersonic Concorde plane has a beautiful silhouette. It flies between Europe and the United States in hours less than normal jet planes.
The Concorde is the most difficult plane in this book, but you may like the challenge. The first steps are the same as for the Glider on page 8.

The first steps are the same as for the Glider on page 8.

You will need
Letter or notebook paper
Ruler, pencil

3 Fold the two slanted edges to the middle crease.

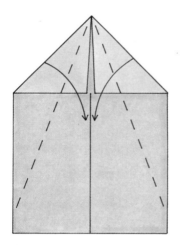

1 Fold the paper in half. Unfold the paper so it lies flat.

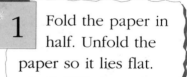

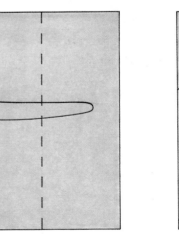

2 Fold the top corners to the crease as shown.

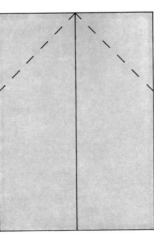

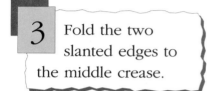

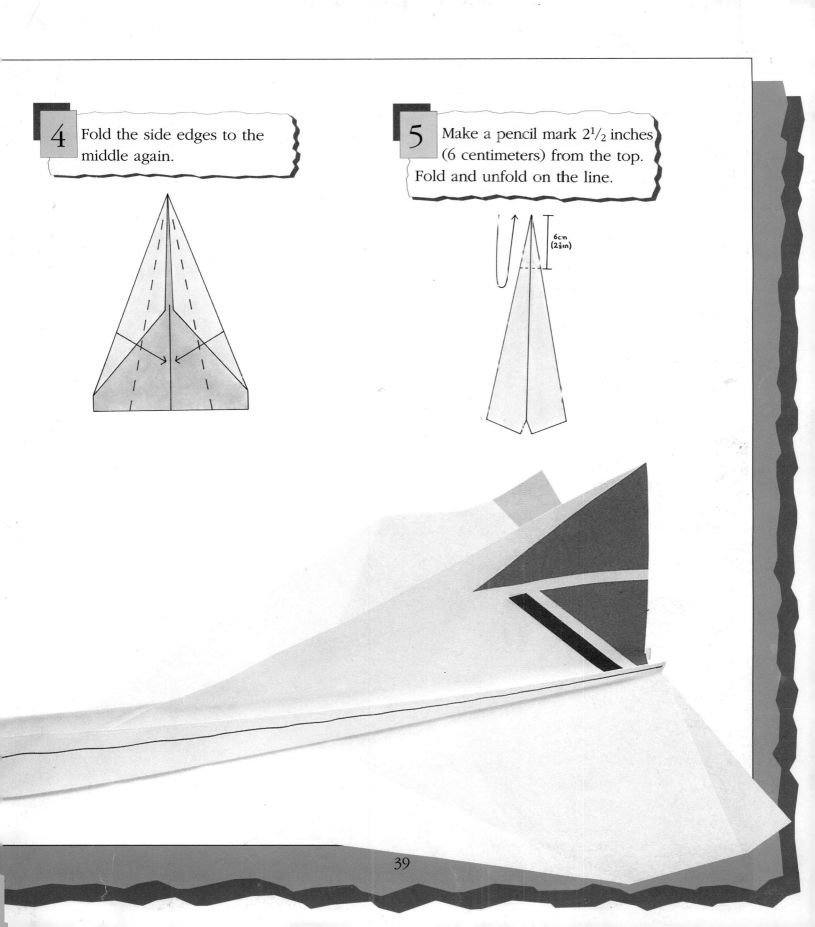

4 Fold the side edges to the middle again.

5 Make a pencil mark 2½ inches (6 centimeters) from the top. Fold and unfold on the line.

6cm
(2½in)

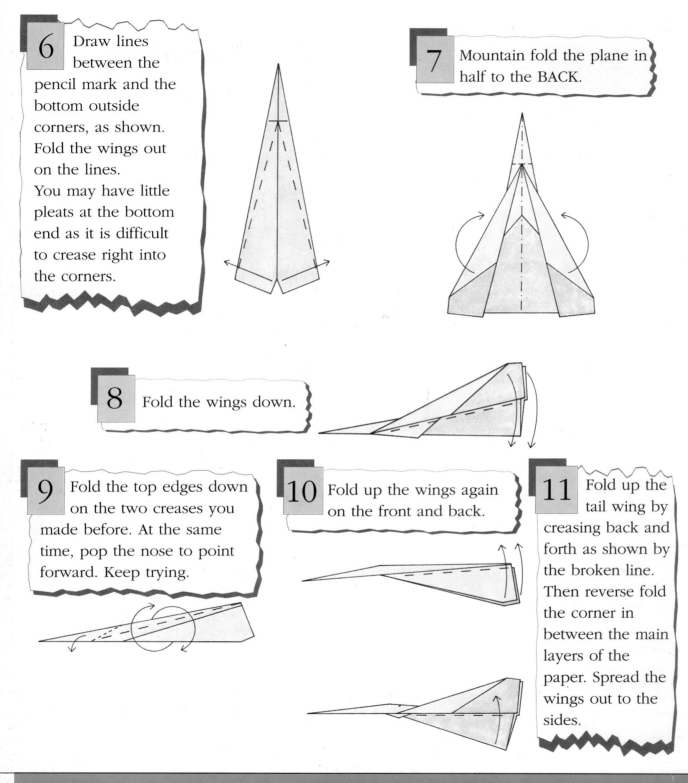

6 Draw lines between the pencil mark and the bottom outside corners, as shown. Fold the wings out on the lines. You may have little pleats at the bottom end as it is difficult to crease right into the corners.

7 Mountain fold the plane in half to the BACK.

8 Fold the wings down.

9 Fold the top edges down on the two creases you made before. At the same time, pop the nose to point forward. Keep trying.

10 Fold up the wings again on the front and back.

11 Fold up the tail wing by creasing back and forth as shown by the broken line. Then reverse fold the corner in between the main layers of the paper. Spread the wings out to the sides.

HIGH FLYER

This plane is one of the smoothest flyers you can make.

You will need
A piece of paper
Tracing paper or
photocopy
Scissors
Paper clip

1 Trace or photocopy the outline of the plane. Cut it out.

2 Fold the plane in half, on the middle line.

3 Fold down both wings.

4 Fold down both rudders. Add the paper clip.

5 Loosen the wings and rudders. Hold the plane under the wings and throw it slightly up.

Flying help
Adjust so that the wings are slightly up and the rudder is slightly down. Experiment with tiny adjustments to the wings and rudder.

6 High Flyer.

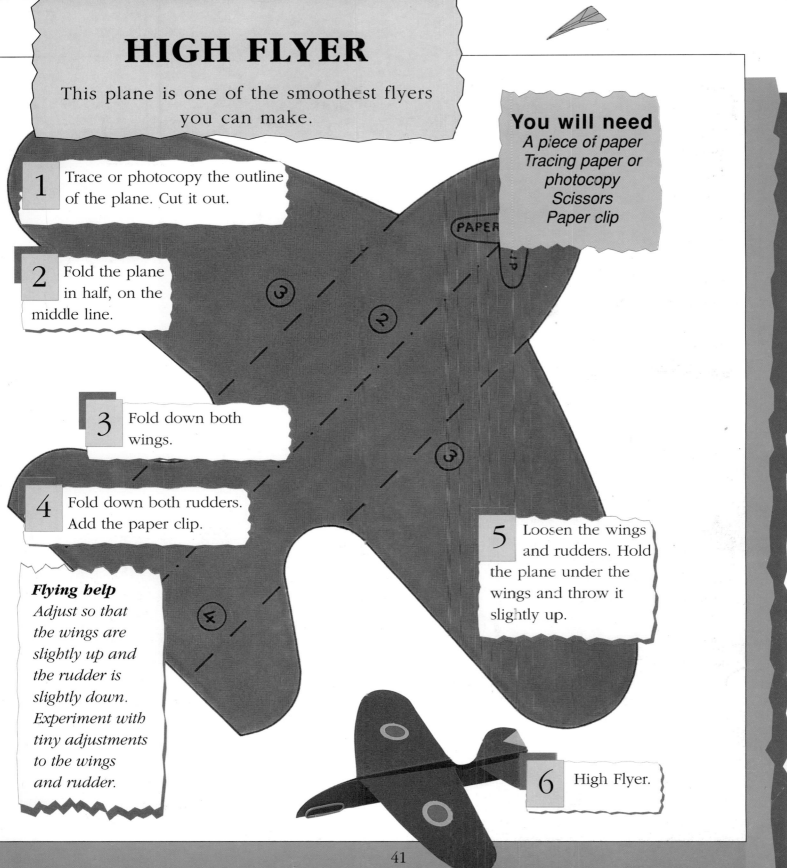

PAPER

KITE

When the wind comes up suddenly, grab a piece of paper and fold it into this simple kite. It flies upside down from the way you might expect, because the narrower corner points up instead of down.
Begin with a square of paper which you can cut from notebook or stationery paper; page 5 shows you how to do it.

page 5 shows you how to do it.

You will need
A paper square
String
Needle
Tissue paper scraps

1 Fold the square piece of paper corner to corner.
Unfold the paper so that it lies flat.

2 Fold the two outer edges to the crease.

Flying tips
Run against the wind, while holding the kite behind you.
Decorations
Bold designs made with colored pens show up the best.

3 Pierce three holes where shown, using a needle (or the point of a pair of scissors). Knot a long piece of string through two holes, leaving a long end for holding the kite in flight.

4 Tie another piece of string to the wide corner of the kite. Cut several pieces of tissue paper 4 x 2 inches (10 x 5 centimeters). Crush them in the middle and tie the tail string around each one.

BUILD AN AIRPORT

You can build a whole airport with just paper and posterboard. Think of all the things you see there: planes, runways, waiting rooms, departure lounges and parking lots, and don't forget people!
Here are some suggestions.

Begin with paper planes in a landing area. Make some paper cars and place them in a parking lot. Then create a large building for your international airport. It could contain big announcement boards, information desks, and baggage carousels.

Pretend you are going on a trip. Build each area that you go through in turn: roads and parking lots, or taxis and buses, the passenger terminal with check-in counters, waiting rooms, and so on.

Pretend you are an architect designing a new airport—make a plan on paper first.

It's up to you to make things simple or complex. For example, you could make cars by folding a piece of paper in half and drawing on the outline. Or you could try to construct little three-dimensional cars with wheels and cut-out windows.

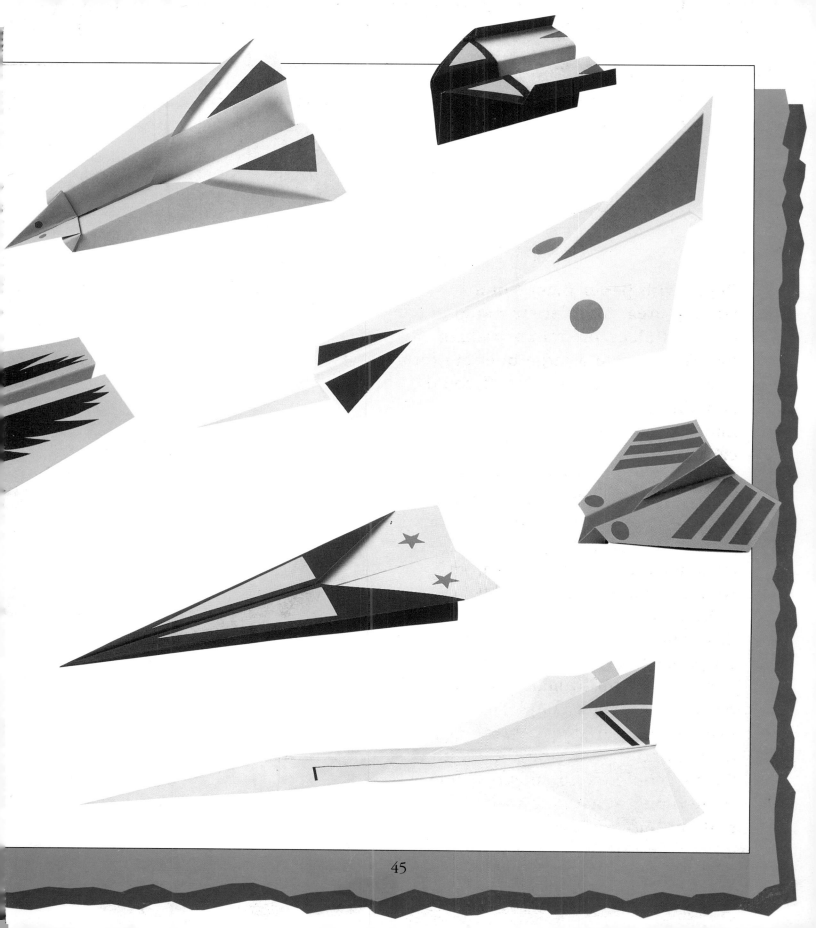